The clearest way into the Universe

is through a forest wilderness.

Quotation Sources

Badè, William Frederic. *The Life and Letters of John Muir*. Boston: Houghton Mifflin, 1924. On page 5.

Muir, John. "In the Sierra Forests," *San Francisco Daily Evening Bulletin*, July 1875. On page 25.

——. Inscription from field journal. July 1, 1867. On page 30.

——. Marginalia in *The Prose Works of Ralph Waldo Emerson*. On page 27.

——. *The Mountains of California*. New York: Century, 1894. On page 30.

——. *The Mountains of California*. Vol. 5, *The Writings of John Muir*. Boston: Houghton Mifflin, 1916. On page 12.

——. *My First Summer in the Sierra*. Boston: Houghton Mifflin, 1911. On pages 14–15, 17–18, 21, 22–24.

——. *Our National Parks*. Boston: Houghton Mifflin, 1901. On pages 6–7, 9, 11, 32.

Wolfe, Linne Marsh, ed. *John of the Mountains: The Unpublished Journals of John Muir*. Boston: Houghton Mifflin, 1938. On pages 1, 9, 12, 29.

Copyright Information

Illustrations copyright © 2020 Giovanni Manna / Edited by Amy Novesky and Kate Riggs
Designed by Rita Marshall / Published in 2020 by Creative Editions / P.O. Box 227,
Mankato, MN 56002 USA / Creative Editions is an imprint of The Creative Company
www.thecreativecompany.us / All rights reserved. No part of the contents of this book
may be reproduced by any means without the written permission of the publisher.
Printed in China / Library of Congress Cataloging-in-Publication Data
Names: Muir, John, author. / Manna, Giovanni, illustrator. / Manaresi, Laura, compiler.
Title: Wilderness: the words of John Muir / by John Muir; illustrated by Giovanni Manna;
selections by Laura Manaresi. Summary: A collection of some of John Muir's most
memorable and inspirational words reminds us of a shared responsibility and inescapable
bond—that all inhabitants of this planet "travel the Milky Way together."
Identifiers: LCCN 2019056672 / ISBN 978-1-56846-347-6 / Subjects: LCSH: Natural history–
United States. Classification: LCC QH104.M845 2020 DDC 508.73–dc23
First edition 9 8 7 6 5 4 3 2 1

wilderness

THE WORDS OF JOHN MUIR

ILLUSTRATED BY GIOVANNI MANNA

SELECTIONS BY LAURA MANARESI

CREATIVE EDITIONS

Only by going alone in silence, without baggage,
can one truly get into the heart of the wilderness.

John Muir (1838–1914) was a Scottish-born naturalist, activist, and writer who devoted his life to exploring, studying, and protecting the wilderness.

Starting in the late 1860s, Muir's wanderlust led him on treks from Kentucky to Florida, then to Cuba and Panama, and finally through California's Sierra Nevadas and Yosemite Valley. When he wasn't walking, he was writing. Although he may have thought "this business of writing books is a long, tiresome, endless job," he kept at it and managed to publish several, along with hundreds of letters and articles.

Still, it was Muir's deep love for the wilderness that he most wanted to convey and which led him to found the environmental organization known as the Sierra Club in 1892. Later, he helped spur the establishment of several national parks during Theodore Roosevelt's administration. Such activities made Muir a fundamental catalyst for the modern environmental movement.

May John of the Mountain's words continue to inspire.

Walk away quietly in any direction and taste the
freedom of the mountaineer. Camp out among the

grasses and gentians of glacial meadows, in craggy

garden nooks full of nature's darlings.

The sun shines not on us but in us.

Climb the mountains and get their good tidings. Nature's peace will flow into you as sunshine flows into trees. The winds will blow their own freshness into you and the storms their energy, while cares will drop off like autumn leaves.

Wander here a whole summer, if you can.... The time will not be taken from the sum of your life. Instead of shortening, it will indefinitely lengthen it and make you truly immortal.

There is no repose like that of the green deep woods. Here grow the wallflower and the violet.

Every morning, arising from the
death of sleep, the happy plants
and all our fellow animal crea-
tures great and small, and even the

rocks, seemed to be shouting,
"Awake, awake, rejoice, rejoice,
come love us and join in our
song. Come! Come!"

Learn to live like the wild animals, ...

... deer in the forest caring for
their young ...

... the strong, well-clad, well-fed bears ...

... the lively throng of squirrels ...

... the blessed birds, great and small, stirring
and sweetening the groves ...

An eagle soaring above a sheer
cliff, where I suppose its nest is,
makes another striking show of
life, and helps to bring to mind

the other people of the
so-called solitude ...
Going to the mountains
is going home.

Between every two pines is a
doorway to a new world.

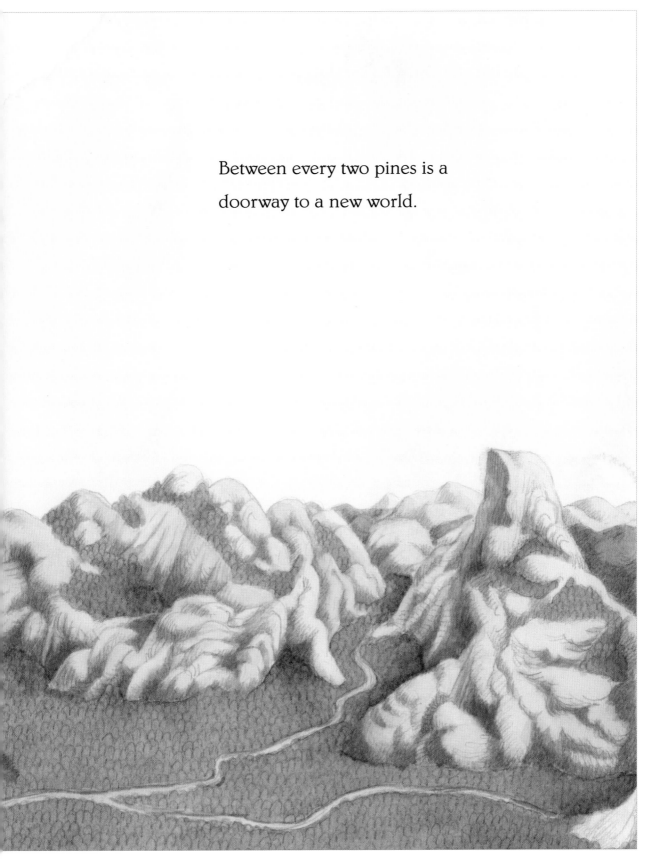

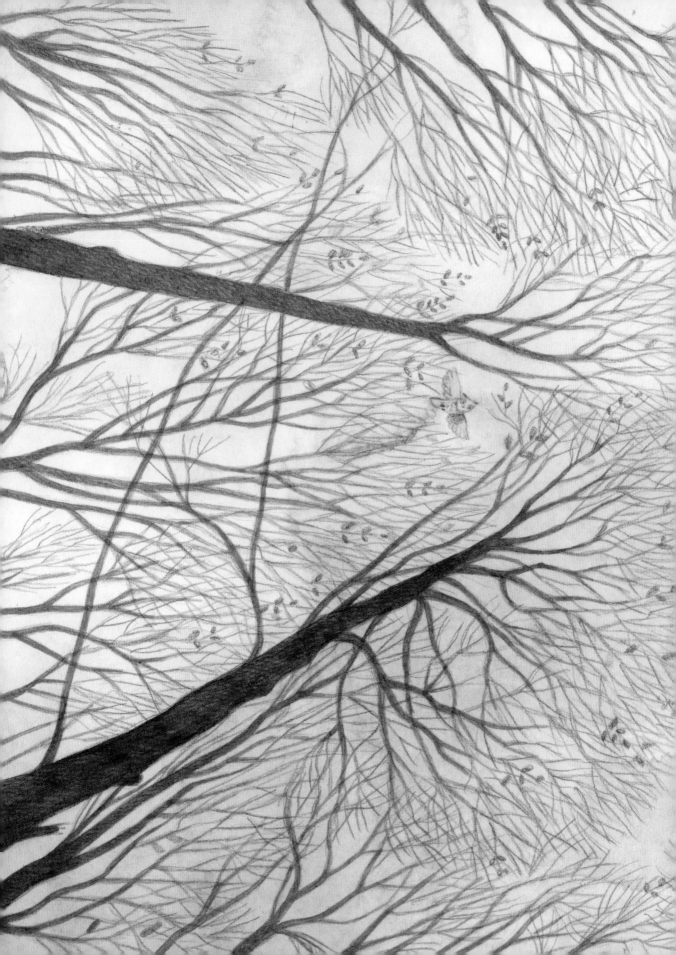

I never saw a discontented tree. They grip the ground as though they liked it, and though fast rooted they travel about as far as we do. They go wandering forth in all directions with every wind, going and coming like ourselves, traveling with us around the sun two million miles a day, and through space heaven knows how fast and far!

We all travel the Milky Way
together, trees and men.

John Muir, Earth Planet, Universe

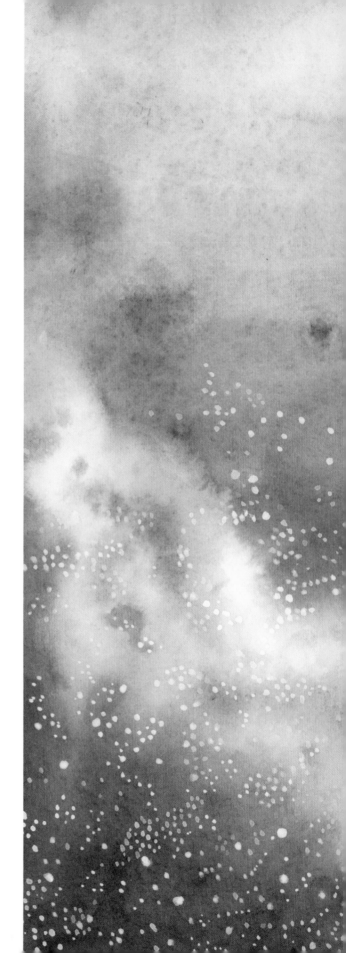

This is Nature's own reservation, and every lover of wildness will rejoice with me that by kindly frost it is so well defended.